Vagabond Heart..

Soumya Mohapatra

Presentation by *BookLeaf Publishing*

Web: www.bookleafpub.com

E-mail: info@bookleafpub.com

ISBN: 9789357217507

First edition 2023

DEDICATION

TO THE SERENDIPITIES OF MY LIFE...

ACKNOWLEDGEMENT

~~ My father who flooded me with books when I'd barely begun to read, knowing the words will guide me on their own...

~~ My mother who urged me to write, as a messenger of my myriad emotions inside, be it to celebrate life, love and hope or as a weapon to chase away distress & fears..

~~ My friends who've been kind enough to read every poem of mine, relating to them, debating or drawing inspiration from them, and encouraging me ..

~~ and of course this vagabond heart of mine that loves to travel the length and breadth of life experiences with all it has, celebrating every emotion with gusto !

PREFACE

Cliched though it may sound, we only have one life to live, and unless we give it our all and get soaked in every color it splashes on us, would it ever feel complete and well-lived?!

As an only child and a studious one, I had limited time & ways to socialise or be entertained at home so books became my buddies, taking me on beautiful escapes from reality. I started connecting to the characters so much I started writing poems about them. I was 14 then and haven't stopped writing ever since.

Little did I know that my own life would go on to be so interesting, every page, every chapter, an experience to savour. And am glad it hasn't been only joyful highs or perfect positives else I dare say I may not have been here.

To me, perfection often is boring, it's the incomplete, the unsaid & the imperfect that makes the cut, the fullness of life, celebrating every pleasure and pain likewise. A confusion, a conflict, a diversion, are what inspire most of my poetry and I feel fulfilled when it not just resonates with someone but also if it doesn't coz I feel the essence of a poem lies in the variety of interpretations & reactions it can elicit.

Magic In You

Theres a storm raging beneath the buoyantly
calm sea,
and a butterfly done being a caterpillar, longing
to be set free..

Theres a gale of wind rustling the trees, craving
to stir it all up happily,
and a madness in that gentle breeze, to keep
dancing crazily..

Theres a bud waiting to bloom while the dewy
garden awaits sunrise,
and a baby shining her brightest in that swarm of
a hundred fireflies..

Theres a streamlet trickling through rocks, that
yearns to be a wild river,
and a little iceblock atop a glacier daring to
plunge into the deep & dark water..

Theres a word aspiring to be in a song, to give
meaning to a melody,
Theres a simple mind working somewhere
turning into a prodigy..

There is in everyone everywhere, a little
something wanting to break free,
Wishing to map new roads, dreaming of new
worlds to see..

It takes but that little fire, that flicker of hope
shining bright,
It takes but that faraway moon to light up a dull
night..

It takes but gorgeous guts to do what you've
simply got to do,
It takes nothing more but a spark of magic in
you...

Set Me Free..or Not..

There may be in everyone everywhere,
a little something wanting to break free,
but also a story of shocks and storms,
striving for a time of normalcy...

There may be hopes soaring high,
even if buried all the way within,
and victories waiting to be captured,
even if coveted on a whim,
but there also are quiet desires in the heart,
sweet simple promises one wants to keep,
a mere flirting with fantasies, a candyfloss
dream and nothing too deep..

There are stars self-driven, hungry forever to
shine and soar,
to aspire & achieve, reach the skies and then
some more..

But content are they too, who live in the now,
breathing in the peace of certainty,
refusing to tread unknown paths,
flourishing in their comforting complacency..

What would I choose, where would I go,

which sky would I fly to meet my dreams,
do I have enough fire to melt the mould,
or am I cheering for the buzz of routine..

In a world full of ties and rules,
do I know what it takes to break a few,
do I really want to set myself free ,
or simply stay & evolve, not start anew...

Set me free, or not, is then how
we confuse a committed me,
oscillating cheerily,
in a world full of ways to let go or just be..

Holding cards up close..

When you speak of them shattering your trust &
faith,
the scars on your heart clouding up your eyes,
when you call their wandering hearts your
helpless fate,
merely going through the motions of your life,
I yearn to be your tree, your rock, your temple of
peace amidst the storm,
hoping you'll see the silver linings,
the receding tears, the purposeful calm..

I pray your prayers are answered,
and you do believe in something,
I wish you realise how fragile is time,
and not forget to live while making a living..

Within you lies a passion so strong,
a soul that knew to love and how,
and around you shines glorious love,
if only you let your then be beaten by your now..

I tell you friend,
from the other side of hope,
it's just a small bridge you've to dare & cross
take that first step and meet up in the middle,
don't hold all your cards up so close..

PostScript

It's a surprise, an absolute surprise and a
delightful one to top it,
When the heavens want to send a windfall, how
on earth can one stop it..

The first smiles, the first hello's had perhaps a
different hope in mind,
But life intervened, distractions convened,
bringing up fences of every kind..

The thoughts raced, chemicals raged,
but the beliefs wavered so much so,
turning a probable happily ever after,
into a fleeting touch and go..

Years flew, we grew,
words flowing across the terrains of time,
a cozy calm, a shared song,
casual talks so soul quenching & sublime..

We get it all, the mad adventures, the daily buzz,
the saga like stories,
We bear it all, the differences, the equations, the
confusing histories..

It's funny to see now, oneself outside, breathing
in another form,
It's weird how one's whackiest thoughts, now get
endorsed as the norm..

It's unbelievable how two persons apart could
grow into each other so seamlessly,
It's nice to feel you've figured out life,
even if momentarily..

The scenes keep flitting,
the times keep turning,
letters from destiny writing out every day,
Thank God for the Post script in you,
a banal life suddenly having something more
beautiful to say!

Again

I wish I could show,
how much I care,
But am so scared,
of all that may happen,
could be a song, the peace lasting long,
Or rub it in wrong, and burn up again..

I wish I could say,
all thats playing,
wiping the weird out and away,
But then I wonder,
isn't this better,
drifting by invisibly day after day ..

I wish I could hear,
the lines unspoken
the words unwritten,
somehow making their way out of you,
your gazes still burn, cooking up a storm
I wish I could look away, I really do..

I wish I could feel
those emotions bizarre,
just doesn't seem fair,
to lose hold of them all of a sudden,

So here I go & dream,
mad as it may seem,
hoping our paths will cross again..

Heartsong

A bounce in the step, a swing in the sway,
feels like spring every other day,
wind kissed hair, a soft warmth in the air,
something keeping the worries at bay..

Music weaving the minds so much,
the heart songs sweetly echoing each other,
a shy smile, a stolen touch,
making the heartbeats run pitter patter!

The skies delight with their hues,
the clouds weaving smoky stories,
the leaves rustle and bustle through,
the trees relishing their histories..

The roads twist and turn,
the sceneries tugging your heart tight,
you don't really need to reach somewhere ,
its already a trip to paradise alright..

Your heart aflutter, your eyes blink in wonder,
these stolen moments from the usual chores,
you look out the window at the dancing tiles of
life,
you look in and live the happiest time of yours..

Fleeting but Eternity..

Fleeting moments of magic, stolen from reality,
When wisdom happily loses to strolls of
insanity,
We'll fly away and apart eventually but that
seems a tiny casualty,
When our banter laughs on merrily, echoing
through our own lil' eternity..

One life..

When you meet someone who puts the stars in
your eyes,
makin' bumpy roads look like bright fluffy skies,
logical and practical are mere words down the
scroll,
when only the moment you meet, your world
finally feels whole..

See your rainbows together even if for a
moment,
cherish the sunbeams of hope and bliss,
Stuff like this ought to be loved, lived & relived

So go all out and savour the heights to which he
makes your wishes fly,
for it is one life, and it is slipping by..

Sunset..

Color me with the Sunset,
caress me with the breeze,
cajole me with promises,
cloak me with the wind..
Ask me to wait here and I will,
calm eyes holding wildness within,
basking now and burning then,
unwavering even if I don't know when,
the shore will come, the anchor will drop,
when two pairs of feet will seek each other,
the sunset will watch the gazes mingle,
tremble with the unsaid,
and a dozen dreams will come alive again..

A blushing memory..

Just a while ago
felt like one of those days,
spent in drunken haze..
I suddenly remember,
what made my heart bloom,
lit a flame dancing wildly,
like waves with the moon..
Mere words by you,
but there they go melting me,
mere smiles from you,
but they are rainbows I see..
This is just a dream, I know,
& only a dream it ought to be,
else such mesmerizing magic ,
could eclipse my reality..
So here we settle down,
my somersaulting heartbeats and me,
letting you and the moment be,
just another blushing memory..

An Elsewhere with You

I remember you'd turn me around,
take my face in your hands,
kiss me, gently at first,
and then blush as much as me..

I remember you'd walk by my side,
counting clouds by day & stars by night,
then brush on my cheek,
your trembling fingers gently..

I remember how we almost became,
what we felt we were meant to be,
& how our world could see,
a naive dream lingering towards reality..

Yet something didn't blend right,
or maybe we can blame distance & time ,
but something wasn't enough,
in me or you or us,
that was enough to drive us apart heartlessly..

An elsewhere with you,
is now just a fleeting memory,
sand trickling through my hands,
swifter than it seems,

the second-hand ticking away on a clock,
its insane to want to make it stop..

An elsewhere with you, though,
is a pain I've learnt to celebrate,
the more it hurts, I turn it to verse,
and call it the glum poetry of fate.

There's no "us" but an amazing US

There's no "us" but an amazing US,
in the love we share, the trust and care,
in the magic we fill in each others air..
in the dreamlands we go together to,
in the troubles we pull each other through,
in the little special things we do & fuss
There's no "Us".. but an amazing US..

I saw you first, in a sliver of sunrays,
little knowing you'll become my sunshine
I felt your shoulder, perhaps in reluctance,
but among strangers, one I could call mine..

Wish I had known you when I had a lot less to
lose,
when I had the guts to take on a tough bet,
when I could dare my wishes to be horses,
and race them boldly against the sunset..

Theres no "us", just an amazing US,
in our roles now, as fated friends,
in the play of words,
the gorgeous emotions,
the games we play in all the realms,
in the buoyant beginnings to the happy ends..

Now you'll never know..

You knew how to love me tender,
how to hold me tight,
You knew how to be my wishing star,
my moonlit night,
You knew how to possess me,
kiss away my doubt,
Oh wish you knew how to stay,
when the embers died down and the flames went
out..

Wish you knew what to do when the going went
tight,
but you chose to give up rather than fight,
you left when it felt like a never-ending dark
night,
so now you'll never know how to bask in my
light..

Wish you showed some heart,
when you claimed I had yours,
wish you'd shared what you feared,
so I'd have cleared it off your path ,
and made it at least midway but together..

Now you'll never know what it is ,

to make mushy mornings for each other,
& fuzzy dreams into somethin' sweetly real,
now you'll never know what it is
to stay young when growing old together,
live a story so warm, a journey so surreal..

By the window..

There's a moment in a day somewhere,
when I will peep out of the window and see you,
waiting, thinking, stealing glances,
wondering if I will look out, catch your eye,
the way I have wondered all these years,
if you really were or if I merely imagined you,
imagined us,
imagined what we called forever,
in butterflies, fires and feelings within..
So till then, I sit by a window,
not waiting, not thinking,
but in imagined longing and real bliss..

Scribbled tale..

You sauntered right in,
as if by right,
turning stranger to friend, in just a few moons,
friend to lover in just one.

Irritating my sensibilities,
mocking my oddities,
enriching my memories;
Each mind of a kind,
Each heart, a quirky work of art;

Have often wondered what made our paths
collide,
our fates entangled, and crossing the decade plus
divide

To plunge into passions unforeseen,
breaking boundaries in every way,
teaching me what's beyond, no matter what it
took,
a burning tale scribbled on my life's scrapbook..

Come home to me..

Someone asked me today what it takes,
to be able to rise after every fall,
to stay up nights & watch mornings unfurl,
to chin up & keep moving on.

I said "Forgiveness & Love",
for Myself,
above everything else,
beyond everyone else..

Hurdles & heartbreaks
exist perhaps for this reason,
in no matter what age or season,
to show me what I am, can do & be..
how I'll figure & fix me
to shine like sunbeams dancing on a choppy
sea..
And hence I know I'd be able to do things I
wouldn't otherwise dare,
make the boldest moves, go anywhere,
I can move up and away, fearlessly
coz I can always come back home to me..

Dreams don't die!

Look at those eyes and you'll know,
dreams don't die, they forever glow,
pausing just a while, they take a step back,
letting life get it's way, cutting it some slack..

But oh how they stay alive, it's almost magic,
in dusty scrapbooks and musty memories,
inside heartsongs and those bonfire stories..

You only need to know where to look,
where to pull them out from,
and soon they'll sparkle again in your eyes,
bravely cutting through the humdrum!

Your Magic..

Sure you have flaws, sure you have lows,
sure you get swayed as the wind blows,
sure you stumble blinded by those tears,
and your heart burns even after all these years..

But pause a while and see, the magic that can be,
if you only let it go, if you only believe,
that running in your veins are bright galaxies,
which shine through your soul,
beam bravely off your face,
making all days perfect days, to just revel in
you,
your magic, your magnificence..

Balancing It

25

I'll walk by your side, lend ears to your sighs,
words will soothe, creases will smoothe,
my shoulders reaching up to hold you,
when you're feeling blue...

And I'll try not to mind, when you turn blind,
to my stormy weather, shutting your shelter,
for you're still trying to make it,
aren't you..

But let me confess, that I smile nevertheless,
even if am tearing up within,
that I do have my share, of life not being fair,
and the going's tougher than it may seem..

I will act like your rainbow,
but need you to hide me from the rain,
for a spot of sunshine I sure am,
but blazing through clouds again & again..

I'll still do anything for you, your smile,
In love or something like that,
but be my anchor, for more than just awhile,
for real, and for balancing this act,
else let me take a step or more back,
to preserve this complicated heart..

Now..

I find it a silly thing, to keep on waiting,
for the right time to start living your life,
how will you know,
where to wake up and go,
if you're always lost in races and strife..

Time won't wait, rolling the dices of fate,
and you've got to grab it with all you have,
dancing with grace and might,
all the way from dawn to twilight,
never regretting a missed chance..

Never stop standing up for yourself,
even if you've to step over a few lines,
Never stop believing you can finish,
even if you've outrun by several miles..
Know that you will fly, there's endless fire
beneath your wings,
Know that living in the now get you guts to face
whatever every tomorrow brings..

What made Me Smile..

Would you believe me if I told you,
I've learnt to live in my own way,
making magic with what I have & who,
and making peace with what I don't,
how promises I heard are fading away,
while the ones I make to myself, won't;

Would you believe me if I told you,
its fine to untie the strings, let it go,
that emotions do get better with time,
and when you let them mingle & flow,
the darkest hours turn slowly sublime;

When you fear less and accept more,
you value what you have,
whats worth fighting for,
then you remember to adore who you are,
treasure yourself for a good while;
Thats the way it worked for me,
the way that made me smile.